UTM SE AND THE FUTURE OF RETRO COMPUTING ON IOS

A Comprehensive Review And
Guide To The First PC Emulator
Approved By Apple For Ios

John Clean

Table of Contents

Introduction

UTM SE, the first PC emulator approved by Apple for iOS, faced initial rejection due to concerns over the app's user experience. However, the UTM SE team collaborated with the AltStore Team to improve the app, providing valuable support and guidance. Apple ultimately approved UTM SE for release on the App Store, making it available for free download on iOS, iPadOS, and visionOS devices. This marks a significant milestone for retro computing on Apple's platforms.

Developed by Turing Software LLC, UTM SE is based on the QEMU emulator and allows users to run classic software and old-school games on their iPhone, iPad, and Apple visionOS devices. It stands out for its versatility, handling various computer architectures such as x86, PPC, and RISC-V. The app supports both graphical operating systems and text-only systems, offering users the flexibility to explore a wide range of vintage software and games.

UTM SE's compatibility extends to iOS 14 and newer versions, iPadOS, and visionOS, making it accessible to a large number of Apple device users. With

UTM SE, enthusiasts can revisit classic computing experiences and delve into the world of retro gaming on their modern Apple devices.

CHAPTER ONE

Key Features of UTM SE

UTM SE, the first PC emulator approved by Apple for iOS, boasts several key features that make it a powerful tool for running classic software and old-school games on iPhone, iPad, and visionOS devices:

Powerful Emulation Engine

UTM SE is built upon QEMU, a widely used and robust open-source emulator. This foundation ensures reliable and efficient emulation of various computer architectures.

Versatile Architecture Support

The app can emulate x86, PPC, and RISC-V architectures, allowing users to run a diverse range of operating systems and software.

Dual Mode Support

UTM SE supports both VGA mode for graphical operating systems and terminal mode for text-only systems. This flexibility enables users to explore a wide variety of vintage software and games.

Customization Options

Users can either use pre-built virtual machines or create their own custom configurations from scratch. This feature offers a balance between convenience and flexibility for those seeking a specific retro computing experience.

With these powerful features, UTM SE opens up new possibilities for iOS users to delve into the world of retro computing and gaming on their Apple devices.

Development and Approval Process

UTM SE, the first PC emulator approved by Apple for iOS, faced an initial rejection from the tech giant before ultimately securing approval:

Initial Rejection by Apple

When UTM SE was first submitted to the App Store, Apple rejected the application. The company cited concerns over the app's user experience, seemingly ending UTM's hopes of bringing the emulator to iOS devices.

Collaboration with AltStore Team

Undeterred, the UTM SE team worked closely with the AltStore team to make improvements to the app. This collaboration proved crucial, as the AltStore team provided valuable support and guidance to the developers.

Pivotal QEMU TCTI Implementation

Another key development was the implementation of QEMU TCTI by a separate developer. This pivotal change was instrumental in helping UTM SE secure Apple's approval.

Final Approval and Availability

After overcoming the initial hurdles, Apple ultimately approved UTM SE for release on the App Store. The emulator is now available for free download on iOS, iPadOS, and visionOS devices, marking a significant milestone for retro computing on Apple's platforms.

The approval of UTM SE demonstrates Apple's willingness to reconsider its stance and accommodate innovative third-party applications that cater to a dedicated user base. This development opens up new possibilities for iOS users to explore classic software and games on their Apple devices.

Retro Computing Possibilities

Retro Computing Possibilities with UTM SE

The approval of UTM SE by Apple opens up exciting possibilities for retro computing enthusiasts to experience classic software and old-school games on their iPhone, iPad, and visionOS devices:

Running Vintage Software and Games

With UTM SE's ability to emulate various computer architectures like x86, PPC, and RISC-V, users can now run a wide range of classic software and old-school games on their modern Apple devices. This includes popular titles from the 80s and 90s that were originally designed for systems like the Apple II, Commodore 64, and DOS PCs.

Exploring Vintage Operating Systems

UTM SE also enables users to delve into the world of vintage operating systems.

From the early days of personal computing, users can now experience the nostalgia of Windows XP, Mac OS 9, and even older systems like DOS on their iOS, iPadOS, and visionOS devices.

Preserving Computing History

The approval of UTM SE by Apple is a significant step in preserving computing history and allowing new generations to experience the evolution of personal computers. By running classic software and exploring vintage operating systems, users can better understand the roots of modern computing and appreciate how far the technology has come.

Potential for Homebrew and Retro-Styled Projects

The availability of UTM SE on Apple platforms may also inspire a new wave of retro computing enthusiasts to explore homebrew and retro-styled projects. With the ability to run emulators on their devices, users can experiment with building their own retro-inspired hardware and software, further expanding the possibilities of retro computing on iOS, iPadOS, and visionOS.

CHAPTER TWO

Customization and Flexibility

Customization and Flexibility with UTM SE

UTM SE offers users a great deal of customization and flexibility when it comes to running classic software and old-school games on their Apple devices:

Creating Custom Virtual Machine Configurations

One of the key features of UTM SE is the ability for users to create their own custom virtual machine configurations.

This allows them to tailor the emulation environment to their specific needs and preferences. Whether it's adjusting the hardware specifications, selecting the desired operating system, or fine-tuning other settings, UTM SE provides the tools for users to build their ideal retro computing setup.

Downloading Pre-Built Machines from the UTM Gallery

For those who don't want to go through the process of building a virtual machine from scratch, UTM SE also offers the option to download pre-built configurations from the UTM gallery. This gallery hosts a collection of virtual machines that have been created and shared by the UTM community. Users can simply select the pre-built machine that suits their needs, whether it's a vintage Windows system, a classic Mac OS, or a retro Linux distribution, and start running it on their Apple device.

The combination of custom configuration options and the availability of pre-built machines gives UTM SE users a great deal of flexibility. They can choose to create their own unique setups or simply download and use the virtual machines that have been curated by the UTM community. This level of customization and choice is a key strength of the UTM SE emulator, allowing users to tailor their retro computing experiences to their individual preferences.

Implications and Impact

Implications and Impact of UTM SE's Approval

The approval of UTM SE, the first PC emulator for iOS, by Apple has several significant implications and impacts:

Expanding the Functionality of iOS Devices

The availability of UTM SE on iOS, iPadOS, and visionOS devices opens up new possibilities for users. They can now run a wide range of classic software, old-school games, and vintage operating systems on their Apple devices, greatly expanding the functionality and versatility of these platforms.

Demonstrating Apple's Willingness to Accommodate Innovative Apps

Apple's decision to approve UTM SE, after initially rejecting it, represents a shift in the company's stance towards emulator applications. This move shows Apple's willingness to reconsider its policies and accommodate innovative third-party apps that cater to a dedicated user base, even if they challenge the traditional boundaries of the iOS ecosystem.

Potential for More Emulator Applications in the Future

The success of UTM SE and Apple's approval of the app could pave the way for more emulator applications to be developed and approved for iOS, iPadOS, and visionOS. This could lead to a broader ecosystem of retro computing and gaming experiences on Apple's platforms, further expanding the possibilities for users.

Overall, the approval of UTM SE is a significant milestone that demonstrates Apple's openness to innovation and its commitment to providing users with a diverse range of experiences on its devices. This development is a win for both retro computing enthusiasts and the broader iOS community, as it unlocks new possibilities and sets the stage for potential future advancements in this space.

Conclusion

The approval of UTM SE, the first PC emulator for iOS, by Apple is a testament to perseverance and collaboration in the tech world. After facing an initial rejection, the UTM SE team worked closely with the AltStore team and other developers to make the necessary improvements, ultimately securing Apple's approval.

This development is a significant win for retro computing fans and the broader iOS community. UTM SE opens up new possibilities for users to experience classic software, old-school games, and vintage operating systems on their iPhone, iPad, and visionOS devices. The app's versatility, customization options, and support for a wide range of computer architectures make it a valuable tool for those seeking a nostalgic computing experience.

Beyond the immediate benefits to retro computing enthusiasts, the approval of UTM SE also demonstrates Apple's willingness to accommodate innovative third-party applications that cater to niche user communities. This shift in the company's stance could pave the way for more emulator apps to be developed and approved for iOS, iPadOS, and visionOS in the future, further expanding the software ecosystem and the range of experiences available to Apple device users.

Overall, the story of UTM SE's journey to the App Store is a testament to the power of perseverance and collaboration in the tech industry. It is a victory for both the dedicated UTM SE team and the broader community of retro computing enthusiasts who can now explore their passion on modern Apple devices.

www.ingramcontent.com/pod-product-compliance
Lightning Source LLC
LaVergne TN
LVHW051651050326
832903LV00034B/4811